A Little Book of Comfort

To...

May God surround you with his love and give you
his comfort and peace.

From...

Isaiah 49:13

Shout for joy, you heavens; rejoice, you earth; burst into song, you mountains! For the LORD comforts his people and will have compassion on his afflicted ones.

(New International Version)

God cares

As you face
tough times and meet
new challenges,

may God
comfort you,
bless you,

encourage you,
direct you,

advise you,
help you,

and show you
the extent of
his loving care.

God, who made the earth and everything in it,
also cares about one single aching heart.

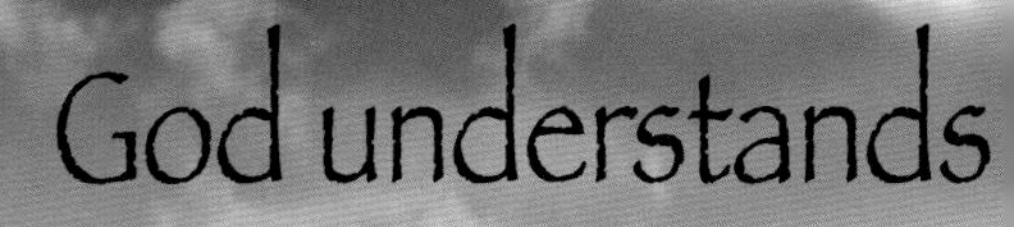

Isaiah 40:31

But those who trust in the LORD will find new strength. They will soar high on wings like eagles. They will run and not grow weary. They will walk and not faint.

(New Living Translation)

James Norton, The Long Climb

Lord Jesus,
Walk beside us when we feel lost.
Give us peace when we are anxious.
Keep us company when we feel lonely.
Comfort us when our hearts are breaking.
Help us cope when life takes a difficult path.
Strengthen us when we are laid low with grief.
Guide us when we don't know which way to turn.
Dry our eyes when we are overwhelmed with tears.
For, because you became fully human,
we know that you understand our feelings now.

God is listening

It's important to pray hardest
when it is hardest to pray.
Anon

Judith Merrell, Hydrangea

Jeremiah 29:12

When you call on me, when you come and pray to me, I'll listen.

(The Message)

Happy times – praise God
Quiet times – worship God
Difficult times – talk to God
Tough times – seek God
Painful times - trust God
All the time – thank God

Prayer has comforted us in sorrow and will help strengthen us for the journey ahead.

George W. Bush
43rd US President, born 1946

God created you

Put your hand over
your heart...
Can you feel your heart beating?
It will beat about 115,000 times today.
God loves you.
He created you.
He set your heart beating.
He cares about you
and your worries.
You are close to his heart.

Psalm 139:14

I praise you because I am fearfully and wonderfully made;

your works are wonderful,
I know that full well.

(New International Version)

God knows what you are going through

Psalm 139:1-6

O LORD, you have examined my heart
and know everything about me.
You know when I sit down or stand up.
You know my thoughts even when I'm far away.
You see me when I travel
and when I rest at home.

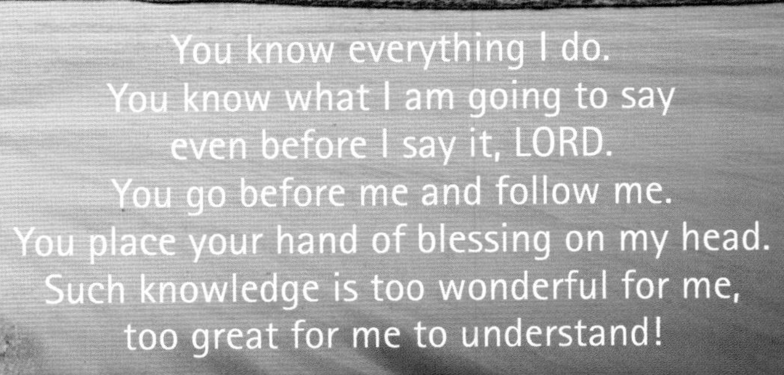

You know everything I do.
You know what I am going to say
even before I say it, LORD.
You go before me and follow me.
You place your hand of blessing on my head.
Such knowledge is too wonderful for me,
too great for me to understand!

(New Living Translation)

Brian Cartwright, Up and Away

God knows how you feel

Lord,
Today, I'm feeling down.
Today, I'm struggling.
Today, life feels grim.

Lord,
Will you lift me up?
Will you encourage me?
Will you give me your peace?

And Lord, may I feel today...

The warmth of your love,
The strength of your protection and
The comfort of your voice.

Take your worries to God

Psalm 55:22

Pile your troubles on GOD's shoulders –
he'll carry your load, he'll help you out.

(The Message)

Matthew 11:28

Come to me, all you who are weary and burdened,
and I will give you rest.

(New International Version)

Philippians 4:6

Don't worry about anything; instead,
pray about everything.

Tell God what you need,
and thank him for all he has done.

(New Living Translation)

A Bible that's falling apart usually belongs
to someone who isn't.
Charles Spurgeon
Baptist preacher, 1834–1892

Jonathan Leach, Poppy

Take your grief to God

Bereavement Prayer

Lord, I feel broken-hearted, bereaved, alone,
I've lost my loved one, a special part of me.
My world has stopped abruptly, ground to a halt,
yet around me life rolls on just as normal.

Lord, give me the strength to start living again.
Help me to cope with this great loss.
Dry my tears when I am overcome with sorrow,
And fill the gap in my life with your love
and peace.

Isaiah 66:13

As a mother comforts her child,
so will I comfort you.

(New International Version)

Brian Cartwright, Two Doves

Spend time with God

Sometimes, Lord, often –
I don't know what to say to you.
But I still come, in quiet
for the comfort of two friends
sitting in silence.
And it's then, Lord, that I learn most from you.
When my mind slows down,
and my heart stops racing.
When I let go and wait in the quiet,
realising that all the things I was going to ask for
you know already.
Then, Lord, without words, in the stillness
you are there...
And I love you.
Lord, teach me to pray.

From *A Silence and a Shouting* by Eddie Askew

Ask God for guidance

A Prayer of St Columba

Dear Lord Jesus,

Be thou a bright flame before me,

Be thou a guiding star above me,

Be thou a smooth path below me,

Be thou a kindly shepherd behind me:

today, tonight, and forever.

St Columba
Irish missionary monk, 521–597 AD

Psalm 142:2–3

I tell you all of my worries and my troubles,
and whenever I feel low, you are there to guide me.

(Contemporary English Version)

Sheila Adams, A Country Walk

God wants to help you

Psalm 32:8

The LORD says,
"I will guide you along the best pathway
for your life.
I will advise you and watch over you."

(New Living Translation)

Isaiah 41:10

"Don't be afraid, for I am with you.
Don't be discouraged, for I am your God.
I will strengthen you and help you.
I will hold you up with my victorious
right hand."

(New Living Translation)

All I have seen teaches me to trust the creator for all I have not seen.

Ralph Waldo Emerson
American writer, 1803–1882

God wants to give you
his peace

May God bless you with peace,
Peace in your heart and peace in your home,
Peace for yourself and peace for your loved ones,
Peace for today's decisions,
Peace for tomorrow's plans,
May God's restoring, reassuring
peace surround you always.

John 14:27
Peace I leave with you; my peace I give you...
Do not let your hearts be troubled and do not be afraid.
(New International Version)

The Lord will either calm your storm... or allow it to
rage while He calms you.
Anon

Peter Topley, Norway

God is on your side

Deuteronomy 3:22

Do not be afraid of them; the LORD your God himself will fight for you.

(New International Version)

Joshua 1:9

Do not be afraid; do not be discouraged, for the LORD your God will be with you wherever you go.

(New International Version)

Psalm 37:39

The LORD protects his people, and they can come to him in times of trouble.

(Contemporary English Version)

God is always the same

Let nothing disturb you,
Let nothing dismay you,
All things pass,
God never changes.

St Teresa of Ávila
Carmelite nun, 1515–1582

Hebrews 13:8

Jesus Christ is the same yesterday and today and for ever.

(New International Version)

Psalm 147:3

He heals the broken-hearted and binds up their wounds.

(New International Version)

When life is blowing up a storm,
make God your anchor.
He won't let you be blown off course.
Charles Kinsey, Tobermory

Nothing is impossible for God

Earth has no sorrow that heaven cannot heal.

Thomas Moore
Irish poet, 1779–1852

Judith Merrell, View from the plane

Nothing can separate us from God's love

Remember...
When you feel sad, God loves you
When you are down-hearted, God loves you.

When you feel depressed, God loves you.
When you are worried, God loves you.

When you feel unwell, God loves you.
When life looks grim, God loves you.

However you feel, Your Father in Heaven loves you
and cares about you.

God is watching over you

Psalm 121:5–8

The LORD himself watches over you!
The LORD stands beside you as your protective shade.
The sun will not harm you by day,
nor the moon at night.

The LORD keeps you from all harm
and watches over your life.
The LORD keeps watch over you as you come and go,
both now and forever.

(New Living Translation)

Psalm 91:11

God will command his angels to
protect you wherever you go.

(Contemporary English Version)

Psalm 91:4

He will cover you with his wings; you will be safe in his care; his faithfulness will protect and defend you.

(Good News Translation)

God will be with you always

Deuteronomy 31:8

The LORD himself goes before you and will be with you;

he will never leave you nor forsake you.

Do not be afraid; do not be discouraged.

(New International Version)

Charles Kinsey, Sunset over Coll from Calgary Bay, Mull

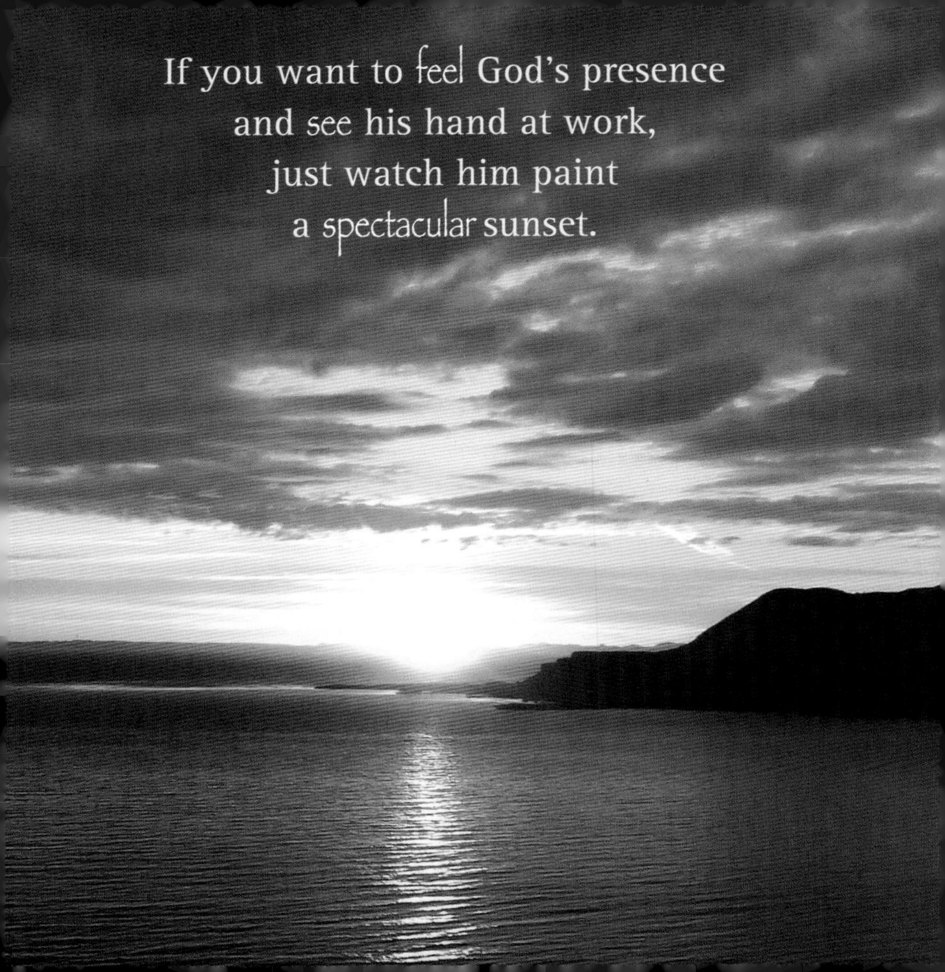

If you want to feel God's presence
and see his hand at work,
just watch him paint
a spectacular sunset.

God wants the best for you

Luke 12:32

My little group of disciples, don't be afraid! Your Father wants to give you the kingdom.

(Contemporary English Version)

Jonathan Leach, Cygnets and Mother Duck and family

Romans 8:28

And we know that in all things God works for the good of those who love him,
who have been called according to his purpose.

(New International Version)

God has good plans for you...

Jeremiah 29:11

"For I know the plans I have for you,"
declares the LORD,
"plans to prosper you and not to harm you,
plans to give you hope and a future."

(New International Version)

What the caterpillar perceives
is the end; to the butterfly is
just the beginning.

Anon

Brian Cartwright, Red Admiral

Heather Hulett, Whitby Abbey

God wants to bless you

As your day begins - May God encourage you.
As your day unfolds - May God protect you.
As your day concludes - May God bless you.
And throughout the night,
May God give you
his comfort, rest and peace.

God wants to comfort you

On sad days,
grim days,
rough days,
rainy days,
anxious days,
stressful days,
pain-filled days,
Lord, please
wrap your loving arms around us,
hold us tight, comfort us,
and fill our hearts with your love
and our minds with your peace.

James Norton, Raindrops on a cobweb

2 Corinthians 1:3–4

Praise be to the God and Father of our Lord Jesus Christ,

the Father of compassion and the God of all comfort, who comforts us in all our troubles,

so that we can comfort those in any trouble with the comfort we ourselves receive from God.

(New International Version)

God often comforts us, not by changing the circumstances of our lives, but by changing our attitude towards them.

S H.B Masterman
Christian leader

Jonathan Merrell, Chatsworth